T0132085

# Didi and Dada

## FRIENDS FOREVER
## AMICI PER SEMPRE

## Maria Alaimo Cinquemani
### Illustrations by Brian Rice

AuthorHouse™
1663 Liberty Drive
Bloomington, IN 47403
www.authorhouse.com
Phone: 833-262-8899

Because of the dynamic nature of the Internet, any web addresses or links contained in this book may have changed
since publication and may no longer be valid. The views expressed in this work are solely those of the author and do
not necessarily reflect the views of the publisher, and the publisher hereby disclaims any responsibility for them.

Any people depicted in stock imagery provided by Getty Images are models,
and such images are being used for illustrative purposes only.
Certain stock imagery © Getty Images.

This book is printed on acid-free paper.

ISBN: 978-1-4685-5586-8 (sc)
ISBN: 978-1-4817-0799-2 (e)

Library of Congress Control Number: 2012903458

Print information available on the last page.

Published by AuthorHouse 12/07/2021

authorHOUSE

## Dedication:

My nieces, my nephews and
To all my wonderful students, who in their
own special way have touched my life.

There once was Didi, a little blue dinosaur.

C'era una volta Didi, un piccolo dinosauro blu.

He lived in a little red house.

Viveva in una piccola casa rossa.

He was lonely, wished he had a friend.
He went out to look for one.

Didi si sentiva solo, desiderava tanto un amico.
Ando` fuori alla ricerca di un amico.

Near the lake between the tall trees, Didi met Dada, a little green dinosaur.

Vicino il lago, tra gli alti alberi, Didi incontra Dada, un piccolo dinosauro verde.

Didi and Dada became best friends.
They started to play together.

Didi e Dada diventarono subito amici.
Giocavano sempre insieme.

They played under the sun,

Giocavano sotto il sole,

in the rain,

con la pioggia

and in the snow.

e anche con la neve.

From the time that Didi and Dada found each other they did not feel lonely anymore and…

Didi e Dada diventarono amici per la pelle e da quel momento…

They are both living together happily
in the little red house.

vivono insieme felici nella piccola casa rossa.

## About the Author

Maria Alaimo Cinquemani has lived in the United States and Italy. For the past 14 years, she has taught Italian to preschoolers and is the preschool coordinator in a prestigious bilingual school in New York City. Her passion and love for teaching and children inspired her to create this book.

"No dream is ever too small, no
dream is ever too big"
-Anonymous-

Printed in the United States
by Baker & Taylor Publisher Services